WEST CHICAGO PUBLIC LIBRARY DISTRICT
3 6653 00150 0671

Life in the World's Biomes

Rain Forest Plants

by Pamela Dell

Consultant:
Ian A. Ramjohn, PhD
Department of Botany and Microbiology
University of Oklahoma
Norman, Oklahoma

Mankato, Minnesota

Bridgestone Books are published by Capstone Press,
151 Good Counsel Drive, P.O. Box 669, Mankato, Minnesota 56002.
www.capstonepress.com

Printed in the United States of America

Library of Congress Cataloging-in-Publication Data
Dell, Pamela.
Rain forest plants / by Pamela Dell.
p. cm.—(Bridgestone Books. Life in the world's biomes)
Summary: "Tells about a variety of rain forest plants, how they are used, why they are in danger, and how they are being protected"—Provided by publisher.
Includes bibliographical references and index.
ISBN 0-7368-4324-8 (hardcover)
1. Rain forest plants—Juvenile literature. I. Title. II. Series: Life in the world's biomes.
QK938.R34D45 2006
581.7'34—dc22 2004029136

Editorial Credits
Amber Bannerman, editor; Jennifer Bergstrom, designer; Kelly Garvin, photo researcher; Scott Thoms, photo editor

Photo Credits
Brand X Pictures, 1
Bruce Coleman Inc./Frithfoto, 16; Janis E. Burger, 20; Laura Riley, 10; Michael Fogden, 4, 6 (bottom right), 6 (top right), 12; Tom Brakefield, 6 (left)
Getty Images Inc./Time Life Pictures/Ovoworks/Bibi Eng, 18
Minden Pictures/Tui De Roy, cover
Peter Arnold Inc./Ron Giling, 14
Tom Stack & Associates Inc./Chip & Jill Isenhart, 8

1 2 3 4 5 6 10 09 08 07 06 05

Table of Contents

Rain Forests

In a tropical rain forest, the air is hot and steamy. Bright flowers and green plants can be seen in every direction. Tropical rain forests are warm year-round. Temperate rain forests, although rare, also exist. They have warm summers and cool winters.

Rain forests get at least 100 inches (254 centimeters) of rain each year. Tropical rain forests lie near the warm **equator**. More kinds of plants grow in tropical rain forests than anywhere else on earth.

◄ A stream runs through an area of thick rain forest in Costa Rica.

Rain Forest Plants

Rain forests have four different layers. The forest floor is the bottom layer. Next is the understory. Higher still is the canopy. The emergent layer is at the top.

Plants grow in all four layers. Though nearly bare, the forest floor holds **moss** and **fungi**. **Ferns** and **shrubs** grow in the rain forest understory. The tops of tall trees press together to form the canopy. Kapok trees grow in the emergent layer. The tops of these trees look like glossy green umbrellas over the canopy.

◄ Trees stretch high in the emergent layer (left). Ferns (top right) and fungi (bottom right) grow close to the ground.

Rain Forest Plant Features

Rain forest plants have different features that help them live. Little sunlight shines through the canopy to the understory. Many understory plants, like heliconias, have large leaves. Large leaves take in more sunlight.

Pouring rains often soak the high forest canopy. Too much rain can hurt the plants. Many rain forest plants have hard, waxy leaves that keep out extra water. Other plant leaves have pointed tips to help extra water drip off.

Some large rain forest plant leaves take in sunlight. Other plant leaves with pointed ends shed extra water.

Homes for Animals

Animals live in each layer of the rain forest. Beetles, ants, and armadillos crawl along the dark forest floor. Jaguars and other big cats hide and sleep beneath the understory's thick brush.

The noisy canopy has the most animal life. Spider monkeys and chimpanzees swing from tree to tree. Toucans, squirrels, and sloths also live in the canopy.

Some animals live in the high emergent layer. Eagles and bats rest in emergent trees.

A jaguar walks beneath the dark, quiet understory in Belize.

Food for Animals

Animals get food from many types of rain forest plants. Canopy trees provide fruit for birds, bats, and insects. Parrots crack nuts with their powerful bills. Bees and hummingbirds drink the **nectar** from colorful flowers. Sloths and orangutans eat plant leaves.

Leaves also provide food for leaf-cutter ants. These ants cut leaves off plants and carry them to their underground nests. They use the leaves to grow fungus gardens in their nests. Later, leaf-cutter ants eat the fungus.

A blue-chested hummingbird drinks nectar from a flower in Costa Rica.

Plants Used by People

Rain forests are filled with plants people use. Seeds from the cacao tree are used to make chocolate. Bananas and pineapples are two fruits that grow in rain forests.

Many rain forest plants have been used to treat sick people. Bark from the cinchona tree contains quinine. Quinine treats **malaria**.

People are finding new plants in rain forests all the time. Thousands of rain forest plants have not yet been recorded.

A woman picks cacao pods that may be used to make cocoa, chocolate, or cocoa butter.

KOMATSU

Plants in Danger

People have cut down more than half of the world's rain forests. Farmers clear rain forests to grow crops and to raise cattle. Loggers chop down trees to get the wood. Some wood, such as mahogany, is used to make furniture.

Plants that are used as medicines are also being destroyed. Periwinkle is one plant that is made into medicine. It is used to treat some **leukemia** patients. Other plants not yet discovered might also help treat sick people. Plants that could save lives are lost forever when rain forests are destroyed.

◀ Loggers in a rain forest haul away trees that have been cut down.

ouch! Your feet hurt my roots.
Please stay on the trail.

Protecting Rain Forest Plants

Some rain forest areas are protected. In these areas, logging and clearing land for farming is controlled. Protected rain forests are sometimes in national parks. People can learn more about rain forests at the parks.

Everyone can help protect rain forests. People can support businesses with plant-friendly products. People can also remind leaders to protect rain forests. When rain forests are saved, plants that may someday save our lives can live.

◀ Signs are one way to let people know rain forests need to be protected.

Amazing Tank Bromeliads

Tank bromeliads are amazing rain forest plants. They get their name from their stiff leaves. Their leaves overlap tightly to form a little tank at the plant's center. The tank catches rain. Then it becomes a tiny pool filled with life.

Small plants with no roots or stems grow in the little bromeliad tanks. Mosquitoes and other insects lay eggs there too. The tanks attract tiny frogs, snails, and crabs. Some creatures live their whole lives inside a bromeliad's tank.

◀ Sometimes animal droppings get stuck inside a bromeliad's tank.

Glossary

equator (i-KWAY-tur)—an imaginary line around the middle of Earth; regions near the equator are usually warm and wet.

fern (FURN)—a plant with feathery leaves and no flowers

fungus (FUHN-guhss)—a type of plant that has no leaves, flowers, or roots; more than one fungus is fungi.

leukemia (loo-KEE-mee-uh)—a form of cancer that affects blood cells

malaria (muh-LAIR-ee-uh)—a serious disease that people get from mosquito bites; malaria causes high fever, chills, and sometimes death.

moss (MAWSS)—a soft, short plant; moss covers damp soil, rocks, and tree trunks.

nectar (NEK-tur)—a sweet liquid in flowers

shrub (SHRUHB)—a plant or bush with woody stems that branch out near the ground

Read More

Greenaway, Theresa. *Jungle.* DK Eyewitness Books. New York: DK Publishing, 2004.

Knight, Tim. *Journey into the Rainforest.* New York: Oxford University Press, 2001.

Internet Sites

FactHound offers a safe, fun way to find Internet sites related to this book. All of the sites on FactHound have been researched by our staff.

Here's how:
1. Visit *www.facthound.com*
2. Type in this special code **0736843248** for age-appropriate sites. Or enter a search word related to this book for a more general search.
3. Click on the **Fetch It** button.

FactHound will fetch the best sites for you!

Index